The Power of
Baking with Mindful Intent

A Collection of Recipes and Practices to Enrich Your Me-Time

Caroline W. Rowe and Dr Susan L. Rowe

The Power of Baking with Mindful Intent
Published by Caroline Rowe

PO Box 117
Hindmarsh, 5007
South Australia

Balboa Press
A Division of Hay House
1663 Liberty Drive
Bloomington, IN 47403
www.balboapress.com
1 (877) 407-4847

ISBN: 978-1-5043-1306-3 (sc)
ISBN: 978-1-5043-1388-9 (e)

A catalogue record for this
book is available from the
National Library of Australia

Words and photos by Caroline Rowe
Words by Susan Rowe
Printed by Digital Print Australia
Design by Green Hill Publishing
Photo page 77 Joseph Guilar, used with permission

Print information available on the last page.

Balboa Press rev. date: 08/27/2018

Thermomix is a registered trademark of Vorwerk International AG (Vorwerk) in Australia and
New Zealand and Thermomix in Australia Pty Ltd (Thermomix in Australia) is its authorised
user and exclusive distributor in Australia and New Zealand of Thermomix machines.

This cookbook and the recipes are the work of the authors alone, who have no association
with Vorwerk or Thermomix in Australia. The recipes are not official recipes which have
been tested by or have the approval, of Vorwerk or Thermomix in Australia.

Foreword

In our early days, we humans ate food, perhaps only to survive. Today, despite our hectic society, we engage in time consuming traditions of preparing and sharing meals because, in addition to surviving, we want to pay attention to, connect with, and share joy with those for whom we love and care. Too often, we are so focused on cooking and caring for others that we forget to cook for ourselves and give joy and love to ourselves. Too often, we think that, "there is no point making something special for just me". In this book, Caroline and Susan suggest the very opposite. They suggest that you deserve the same care that you give to others. They propose that you are worthy of being paid attention to also. They endeavour to help you value and love yourself by bringing together self-care focused mindfulness with one of your favourite activities, cooking.

Helping people understand, value, and practice psychological self-care has been the focus of my work as a clinical psychologist, university lecturer, and scientist for over a decade now. For these reasons I am delighted to support this collection of recipes and mindfulness practices that encourage you to value yourself by taking me-time. This book aims to provide you with a healthy approach to paying attention to your feelings, acknowledging them, and supporting yourself during times of emotional upset. This book emphasises the need for me-time with a collection of delicious cakes to enjoy just4You and it encourages you to take care of your mind and emotions using strategies taught in mindfulness. I want to thank Caroline and Susan for creating this book and for sharing the importance of self-care with you.

I hope that you enjoy this collection of recipes and mindfulness practices and that through this book you can develop good self-care practices in your life.

Asst. Prof Siavash Bandarian Balooch
Clinical Psychologist
BPsy(Hons), PhD(Clinical Psychology), MAPS

Acknowledgements

Mum, thank you for not being a
cook or baker but always supporting
me to follow my dreams.

Wendy, for believing in my
vision and keeping me on
track to bring it to reality.

Mozz and AK, for your attention
to the details and honest feedback.

To all my bake testers, taste testers
and proof readers a massive thank
you as without your help this
project would still be a dream.

Contents

Do you cook for a small household? Just you or you and the other half? I do. And have for most of my life.

I've always loved cooking and was active in the kitchen from a young age as my mother hated cooking and never baked. Despite this, my parents entertained a lot. This gave me the chance to be the cook when it came to preparing food for their many social events.

I so loved cooking that the excitement of receiving an honour at the year-end school assembly was completely overshadowed by the fact that it came with a book voucher that allowed me to purchase the, then very expensive and very popular, *Complete Australian and New Zealand Cookbook*. I still have and refer to this book even now. My passion for cooking continues to this day and so too does my collecting of cookbooks.

Over the years I have created dozens of reasons to cook up a storm for friends and family - any excuse to try new and different recipes. I loved throwing a dinner party and would go all out preparing grand spreads for my friends. I delighted in creating dazzling menus and setting beautiful tables. I had, by then, collected elegant dinner sets with all the trimmings to serve twelve with everything matching. I loved it. My friends and family did too.

In 2011 my world changed in an unexpected way. I bought a Thermomix - an amazing kitchen appliance. It helped me to become an even better cook and this inspired me to become a Thermomix consultant. But that was not the change that rocked me. My consultant training required me to practise making the demonstration dishes until I knew them by heart, which took some considerable time. Each dish served six people, so every time I practised a dish at home I would have to eat the leftovers for the next five days. I began to think that there had to be recipes for small households. However, extensive searching found very few. Was I the only person who cooked just for myself?

The answer to that question came as a great shock. In my work at that time I happened across a report, from the recent census, on Australian household sizes. Nearly 60% of all households were either one or two-person households; with one-person households making up almost a quarter of all Australian households. I was not alone! In the USA, the UK and New Zealand the proportion of small households is similar to Australia. Yet most cookbooks catered for four, six or eight people. I felt like I was part of a 'hidden majority'.

This realisation of a 'hidden majority' led me to a lot of reflection on the challenges of cooking for small households. I realised that to prevent food waste, over eating and a freezer full of five or more portions of the dinner I'd just had, I needed to do things differently. The first step was to do the numbers and create recipes sized just for me. This led to my blog, www.cookingjust4me.com, and then working with Thermomix to create the highly successful *Cooking for Me and You* cookbook of recipes for one and two, focused on everyday meals.

My attention then turned to baking. I often wanted a little something to go with my cuppa but I didn't bake as there was just me and I felt, at that time, that it wasn't worth the effort. Besides, cake recipes usually fed eight to twelve people. If I was to treat myself I needed to find recipes that made cakes just4Me. Again, my searching drew a blank. Always one for a challenge, I started a crusade to find the perfect cake to go with a cuppa, sized just4Me - one that was easy to make, even for a non-baker.

Three years of reading, baking, testing recipes, talking to cake bakers, and attending baking classes resulted in a great collection of cakes sized just4Me plus a little for you. Having learned an enormous amount about baking for small households - and creating a considerable collection of great cake recipes - my friends wanted me to share my knowledge. This led to the creation of the www.just4meBakeClub.com, an online cooking school.

During the journey of creating this online business I began to value my quiet moments of me-time. Sitting in the garden with a cuppa and a slice of my homemade cake I realised that these times, where I was just 'in the moment', became a powerful recharge for me, giving me the energy and resilience to enjoy the creative process of building an online business myself. I realised I needed to practise self-care because if I didn't look after me, who would? The more I chose to bake with this in-the-moment focus the more joy I took from what I did and the more I accomplished. Mindfulness was helping me to achieve my vision of an online baking school for those who cook for themselves.

With such a range of cake recipes I was often asked which was my favourite? The answer varied, depending on how I felt at the time. If I needed me-time because I was feeling overwhelmed I knew my favourite was Lemon and Almond Cake from Santiago. If I needed a recharge it was Half Orange Butter Cake. In my head I had this little matrix of cakes and feelings that helped me pick how I was going to care for myself in my me-time. This book is a hardcopy of that mental list.

My niece, Susan, was part of my recipe-testing team, and in addition to giving great feedback on the constant stream of cake recipes I sent her, listened with understanding to my stories of why this or that cake was important to me emotionally. In her professional life Susan is a psychologist, and she generously supported me in my project of passion, encouraging me to champion the importance of self-care.

And that is how we came to create this book. My mission is to encourage small households to value themselves by taking me-time with a little home baked treat, and Susan supports each recipe with a mindfulness exercise that can easily be practiced in everyday situations.

This book is my list of cakes and feelings. It can be used simply as a recipe book, full of beautiful cakes to enjoy just 4You, or as a mindfulness guide for discovering how easy it is to enrich your daily routine with the power of being in the moment. Combine the two, and discover how baking with mindful intent can truly enrich your me-time. Enjoy, because you are worth the effort!

About Mindfulness

By Dr Susan L. Rowe

As a psychologist I know that good mental health involves daily habits of self-care. So often we attend to things which we believe are more important than our emotional health, such as work, the news feed, cleaning our home, or our physical appearance. This is something I have learned from my patients over the past 11 years and from personal experience.

In my various roles as a psychologist it is all too common to see patients in therapy with difficulties that result from a lack of positive regard for themselves and a diminished desire to truly care for themselves. Genuine self-compassion and self-care takes place in the small moments and is something that happens within us. It does not require planning, preparation or money. It is simply caring enough to be still, take the pressure off, and delight in life. This is what mindfulness can teach us.

An Introduction to Mindfulness

I learned the practice of mindfulness through *Mindfulness-Based Stress Reduction*, an approach to mindfulness founded by Dr Jon Kabat-Zinn at the Center for Mindfulness at University of Massachusetts Memorial Medical Center. Mindfulness originates from the Buddhist tradition of developing greater awareness and helping people to learn to live each moment of their lives fully. As a form of meditation, mindfulness involves focusing on the thoughts, sensations or discomforts that occur in the moment, as opposed to trying to distract from these experiences as is taught in other forms of meditation.

This is a very valuable skill in learning to take care of ourselves during times of distress. In mindfulness practice we learn to acknowledge the unavoidable reality of our emotions in the present, learn to face and accept our experience of emotions without tension or resistance, and develop a nurturing relationship with ourselves in which we take care of ourselves during times of difficulty.

Baking with Mindful Intent

Following my Aunty Caroline's journey of me-time and *Cooking just4me+you* I saw that she had found a way to show consideration and care for herself and a wonderful way to encourage others to do the same.

In Cooking just4me+you Caroline captures the essence of self-care: you are worth it because you are you, not because you are a family of four, not because you should reward yourself, but simply that each day and each moment is an opportunity to care for yourself. This care can be found in a piece of cake and a cuppa. So, when Caroline came to me with the idea of writing a book with the purpose of teaching people how to take me-time to bake for themselves and to learn emotional self-care, I was thrilled to be involved.

A Guide to Practicing Mindfulness

Within this book we have provided you with 12 practices of mindfulness, as examples of how you can start to give yourself some more me-time each day. Each of the practices are written to compliment your me-time of baking, however, they are skills you can also apply to your everyday activities. Here are some general tips to keep in mind when doing your mindfulness practices.

1. Mindfulness has been shown to have a therapeutic effect (see Resources – Mindfulness for further reading) however, it should not be used as a replacement for care from a health professional. If you are experiencing symptoms of anxiety, depression, stress, grief or emotional ups and downs that lasts for more than two weeks be sure to see your General Practitioner or contact one of the help services listed in Mindful Resouces (page 78).

2. Mindfulness can help to reduce tension: however, if at any time during your practice you notice sensations of distress, such as rapid breathing, nausea, or a sense of being overwhelmed, it is important to take care of yourself in that moment. Open your eyes, focus on an object in the room and take slow, deep breaths until you feel the distress pass.

3. Try your new-found skills of mindfulness each day: when you clean your teeth, when you are cooking, when you are driving, when you are walking to work. Remember, you can also practice mindfulness while enjoying your slice of cake with a cuppa throughout the week until the cake is finished!

4. During your practices, you can find a comfortable position sitting cross legged, in a chair, lying down, kneeling or in any other position you find comfortable. Make adaptions to the exercises as you need to - remember it is about paying attention to you, not trying to be perfect.

5. At the end of each practice, take a moment to reflect on what you noticed, how you felt, insights you gained and how you feel now compared to when you began the practice. Reflecting on our experiences is an important part of spending time paying attention to ourselves.

About Baking just4Me+you

By Caroline W. Rowe

How I went from being a non-baker to running an online bake club.

I was not a baker. I was a good cook and had written a recipe book, but I didn't consider myself a baker. As much as I loved cakes and baked goods, the thought of making them at home was something that seemed way too hard for me. It was something others did, people who had the magic baking touch.

Baking is described by many as both an art and a science. A mysterious mix that, as a non-baker, put fear in me. Despite this, I still wanted a little something to go with my cuppa. I wanted a small bit of homemade cake, and I didn't want a family sized version that I'd either waste, overeat or stuff in the freezer for another day that never came. Why should I miss out on a home-baked treat just because I was a household of one? Steeled with a resolve to balance the ledger for small households, I started on my crusade to learn how to bake and find my perfect me-time cake, sized for me.

Four years on and I'm in love with baking. The fear has been replaced with joy. I now take great delight in making my own me-time treats or cakes to share with others. I have embraced the art and science of baking and wonder at the magic I create by taking such ordinary ingredients as flour, eggs, and butter and turning them into beautiful just4Me cakes.

In this book I'm sharing my favourite twelve cake recipes and five toppings that make my me-time special. They are ones that you may know well, like Mississippi Mud Cake, and Date and Walnut Loaf, and maybe some new ones, like Sweet Potato, Maple and Pecan Cake or Toscatårta. They are all sized for small households, and I've updated them to match modern, healthy eating standards. They are tasty and rewarding to eat plus easy to make. To me, they are twelve recipes that every small household baker needs to master to have an ample supply of treats to go with their me-time.

Finding the right cake tin – size matters!

The first issue I resolved on my journey was the matter of what was the right size to scale my cake recipes. After lots of research and testing, I decided that the perfect sizes were a 15 cm /6 inch round, and a 15 x 9.5 x 6.5 cm loaf tin. They look like a regular cake and you can get at least six slices from each. So there's enough to share or to have later in the week, and they are not so big that you waste cake.

Finding these tins was challenging, as standard cake tin sizes have increased over time as part of our supersized world. I hunted online, in cooking shops, in op shops at home and overseas while on holidays, with the result that I now have a vast collection of wrong-sized cake tins and two of the right size. I just needed to know where to look. Suppliers are listed in Resources - Baking, at the back of the book.

All the recipes in this book are sized for 15 cm /6 inch round and 15 x 9.5 x 6.5 cm loaf tins.

What's the perfect cake?

Cake size decided, the next challenge was to determine which cakes to make. Which cake is the perfect one to go with a cuppa? Fruitcake? Butter cake? Chocolate cake?

After years of research and testing, my answer is, "It depends on how you're feeling." Hence, this collection of cakes.

But in deciding which cakes got into my collection, I realised that I needed some rules for evaluating which cakes were worthy of my list. What makes a great cake? In my view, I was looking for those that:

Caroline's criteria for just4Me cakes

- Contain a lot less sugar or use lower GI sugar choices.
- Use everyday ingredients that I have in my pantry and use often.
- Use more wholesome flours or are gluten-free.
- Cut well and don't disintegrate into crumbs when eaten.

- Keep well, so there is still some cake for later in the week.
- Delight me and make me feel special when I have some.
- And most importantly, can be made by a busy, inexperienced non-baker.

All the cakes in my cake collection, both in this book and in the just4Me Bake Club, meet these criteria.

Three styles of cake dressing

Size and type of cake sorted, I realised that I had one more step to decide - toppings. Even though my goal was to make healthy, everyday cakes, I also eat with my eyes, and I wanted cakes that looked attractive and tempting. As I don't like eating sugary frostings and fancy icings nor have the time to fuss with them, I needed a different way to make my cakes tempting to my eyes.

My solution was to embrace a wide range of dressings that I think of in three ways. If the cake is for my weekly use as a me-time cake, as most of my baking is, I'll use an Everyday dressing. If I'm planning to share the cake with a friend or I'm taking it to Book Club I'll often use a dressing from my Company's Coming list. If I'm making a celebration cake, I'll opt for one of the Party Time dressing options. Same cake but dressed up differently. Most of the time I dress my cakes for everyday, but as I'm now confident enough to offer to be the birthday baker in my group of friends, I enjoy dressing the chosen cake in its party mode.

Everyday: Topped with nuts or fruit before going into the oven or dusted with either icing sugar, cocoa powder or butter, sugar and cinnamon or my fast chocolate topping, after the cake is baked.

Company's Coming: Drizzle icing, lemon glaze, my fast chocolate topping, roughly spread chocolate ganache or white chocolate, cream cheese topping

Party Time: Chocolate ganache with a smooth glaze or piped white chocolate, cream cheese topping decorated with store bought chocolates or berries.

Six things I've learnt about the art and science of baking for small households

Finally, a list of the things I wish I had known when I started my crusade.

1. Temperature matters with eggs and butter. If the recipe says room temperature, that means at least 30 minutes in a room at 21°C. Temperature affects the way the ingredients mix and the trapping of air in the cake. This is part of the science of baking.

2. Pre-heating your oven is important. Ovens can take up to 30 minutes to reach the desired temperature. Oven gauges are never accurate, so I recommend buying an oven thermometer. I always use the non-fan setting when baking but have also listed the temperature for fan forced. Check how the cake bakes in your oven and note any differences. In my experience, every oven is unique; you just need to take some time to understand it.

3. Take the time to line your cake tin - it makes a difference. The five minutes of time at the start is well worth the investment as it ensures you can easily remove your cake after baking. I use reusable silicon linings that I have pre-cut to fit my two tins. I've listed stockists in Resources - Baking, at the back of the book.

4. Recipe baking time is a guide only. This is part of the art bit of baking. Use your eyes, nose and touch to tell when your cake is cooked. Check five minutes before the end of the suggested cooking time.

5. Follow the recipe exactly the first time you make the cake to see what happens in your environment. Then, if you prefer, mix things your way.

6. Scaling a recipe is not as straightforward as halving or doubling the ingredient quantities. This, I have painfully learnt, requires both art and science. I've made a lot of not-quite-so-wonderful versions of these recipes in order to establish the right one for you. Enjoy!

the Feelings Matrix

Here's my list of favourite cakes and the feelings I most often notice that I'm experiencing when I decide I need to bake them. To help me gain more from my me-time Susan has matched mindfulness exercises to each cake to address that feeling.

The feelings and mindfulness exercises go together but you choose which cake you bake. Enjoy your cake and me-time mindfully because 'just Me' matters!

I need to take me-time as I'm feeling....

Feeling	Cake	Mindfulness exercise
Unloved	Butter Cake	Mindful self-compassion moment
In need of inspiration	Torta Caprese – Flourless Chocolate Cake	Mindfully enjoying
Tearful and in need of a reminder that the world is OK	Traditional Boiled Fruitcake	Mindful wisdom: I Am Enough
The need to calm down	'Hello Ginger!' Cake	Mindful emotions
In need of a reward	Jane's Best-Ever Mississippi Chocolate Mud Cake	A moment of gratitude
Wronged	Date and Walnut Loaf	Object mindfulness
Insecure/anxious	Jubilee Cake	Noticing anxiety: Mindful body scan
Drained, a bit flat/low	Sweet Potato, Maple and Pecan Cake	Sit and let it bake: Sitting meditation
Unworthy	Toscatårta – Almond Caramel Topped Butter Cake	My inner critic is a perfectionist: compassion and mindfulness
Overwhelmed	Lemon and Almond Cake From Santiago	Tune in, pay attention, and choose: The magic quarter second
In need of a recharge/renewed energy	Half Orange Butter Cake	Mindfulness of the senses
Lonely	Coconut and Rum Kuranda Cake with Rum Syrup	Stop and smell the roses: Walking mindfulness

Butter Cake

This is the cake I think of first when I think cake.
I call it Butter Cake and it's the cake that puts
its arms around me to tell me the world is OK.

The same cake in the USA is called Pound Cake and
in the UK they call it a Victoria Sponge, though it is
nothing like what we know of as a sponge in Australia.

This is a light, fine textured cake with an even crumb
and is truly luscious due to the high ration of butter.

The name, Pound Cake, comes from the ratio of
ingredients: 1 pound each of butter, sugar, eggs and
flour.

I've used a method, pioneered by American baker and
cookbook author, Rose Levy Beranbaum, that changes
the usual cake-making sequence. It's easier, and
produces a beautiful, moist crumbed cake. However,
using this method, it's especially important that eggs
and butter are at room temperature (about 30 minutes
in a room of at least 21°C).

Served plain, topped with butter and cinnamon, or a
tangy, lemon drizzle icing, this is a truly comforting
cake.

Butter Cake - Thermomix

Makes one 15 cm x 9.5 cm x 6.5 cm loaf cake
Serves: 6 slices

Ingredients

110 g sugar

110 g plain flour

1 teaspoon baking powder

½ teaspoon salt

110 g unsalted butter, diced, at
    room temperature

2 eggs, at room temperature

¾ teaspoon vanilla paste

Method

Preheat oven **180°C** non-fan forced (**160°C** fan forced). Grease and line a 15 cm x 9.5 cm x 6.5 cm loaf tin, and set aside.

Place sugar in bowl, and mill **5 sec/speed 10**. Scrape down sides.

Add flour, baking powder and salt, and mix **5 sec/speed 4**.

Add butter, and whisk **30 sec/speed 4**. Scrape down sides.

Insert butterfly and add eggs and vanilla paste, then mix **30 sec/ speed 4**.

Pour batter into prepared tin. Scoop out the centre a little to make an indentation. This helps the top to be a bit flatter, as the centre of this cake rises more than the rest.

Bake for **45-50 minutes**. The cake is cooked when a skewer inserted into the centre of the cake comes out clean.

Leave to cool in tin for **15 minutes** then turn onto wire rack until completely cooled.

When cool, cover the top of the cake with your icing of choice, such as *Lemon Drizzle Icing*, allowing it to run down the sides.
Recipe: page 73.

If using cinnamon topping, top while cake is still warm.

Serve plain or with butter.

Butter Cake - Conventional

Makes one 15 cm x 9.5 cm x 6.5 cm loaf cake
Serves: 6 slices

Ingredients

110 g sugar

110 g plain flour

1 teaspoon baking powder

½ teaspoon salt

110 g unsalted butter, diced, at
   room temperature

2 eggs, at room temperature

¾ teaspoon vanilla paste

Method

Preheat oven **180°C** non-fan forced (**160°C** fan forced). Grease and line a 15 cm x 9.5 cm x 6.5 cm loaf tin, and set aside.

Place sugar, flour, baking powder and salt into a bowl, and mix briefly with beaters to incorporate all dry ingredients.

Add butter, and mix slowly at first, then at a medium speed until a cream consistency is achieved.

Add eggs, one at a time, then vanilla paste, and continue to beat until a pale, creamy consistency is achieved.

Pour batter into prepared tin. Scoop out the centre a little to make an indentation. This helps the top to be a bit flatter, as the centre of this cake rises more than the rest

Bake for **45-50 minutes**. Cake is cooked when a skewer inserted into the centre of the cake comes out clean.

Leave to cool in tin for **15 minutes** then turn onto wire rack until completely cooled.

When cool, cover the top of the cake with your icing of choice, such as *Lemon Drizzle Icing*, allowing it to run down the sides. Recipe: page 73.

If using Cinnamon topping, top while cake is still warm.

Serve plain or with butter.

Mindful Self-Compassion Moment

Our first mindful moment is a practice that is at the heart of me-time, and what it means to bake mindfully: care must begin with self-care. It is far too common that we are self-neglectful, particularly when it comes to showing care for ourselves.

Often, we think that it is selfish to be caring towards ourselves, that care is only for others, or that we should feel shame for taking time to reinvigorate ourselves. These are destructive, harsh and untrue ideas. Self-neglect never equals more care: it removes our ability to share love and connection with others and only results in resentment, burn-out and feelings of worthlessness. This meditation is designed to help you practice focusing love and compassion towards yourself, and is a variation on the Metta Sutta prayer or loving-kindness prayer.

Before you start your Butter Cake, take a mindful moment to do this practice. Find a comfortable position, sitting or lying down. Let your eyes close and begin to notice your breathing. Notice the air flow in, and flow out.

Do not change your breathing; simply focus your attention on your breathing. Be curious with your attention and just "notice" your breath. Your attention will likely wander, that is ok. When you notice it wander, just gently focus it back on your breathing.

Gently place your hand over your heart to remind you that our focus is to direct care inwards. With compassion and genuine care for yourself, speak these words out loud:

> *I deserve to be happy, healthy and whole.*
>
> *I deserve love, warmth and affection.*
>
> *I deserve to be protected from harm, and free from fear.*
>
> *I deserve to be alive, engaged and joyful.*
>
> *I deserve inner peace.*
>
> *I deserve to share my inner peace with those I meet.*

As you say these words, be curious about how you respond. There is no need to react or respond, just simply notice how your body, heart and mind respond. Perhaps you'll notice that these words resonate with you. Perhaps you'll notice that part of you wants to reject these words. Perhaps you'll notice that part of you finds these words painful. With kindness and compassion just notice how these words of care feel. Allow the words to take up space, to fill your being, if only for this one moment.

Whenever you notice that your mind has wandered, with gentle compassion, refocus your attention on your breath, your hand on your heart, and your words of self-compassion. Take a deep breath and begin to notice your whole body. Wriggle your hands and feet. Before opening your eyes, take a moment to breathe in the words of self-compassion again and the feeling of being able to take a moment to express your genuine self-care.

Release your hand and gently open your eyes. Take your peace and words of self-compassion with you as you prepare your Butter Cake and produce this delicious buttery treat.

Torta Caprese - Flourless Chocolate Cake

Torta Caprese is a traditional, Italian chocolate and almond cake, named for the island of Capri from where it originates.

A popular cake, it is easy to make. Simply dress it with a dusting of icing sugar for a midweek cake when you need a little chocolatey taste to inspire you. Or dress it up with a coating of rich chocolate ganache and you have a special occasion cake.

This cake keeps wonderfully well in an airtight container on the bench, and a little slice is all I need to be uplifted and inspired on a busy day.

Torta Caprese - Flourless Chocolate Cake - Thermomix

Makes one 15 cm round cake | Serves: 6-8 slices
Gluten free

Ingredients

80 g dark chocolate, broken into pieces

80 g almonds

50 g unsalted butter, diced, at room temperature

50 g sugar

2 eggs, at room temperature

2 teaspoon baking powder

2 teaspoon cocoa powder

1 tablespoon almond or coffee liqueur or strong coffee (optional)

2 teaspoon icing sugar or cocoa for dusting

Method

Preheat oven **180°C** non-fan (**160°C** fan forced). Grease and line 15 cm round, spring form/loose bottom cake tin, and set aside. If not using a loose bottom tin, ensure that the lining extends up the side of the tin to allow easy removal of cooked cake.

Place chocolate in bowl, and grate **8 sec/speed 9**. Set aside.

Place almonds in bowl, and chop **4 sec/speed 6**. Set aside with reserved grated chocolate.

Place unsalted butter, sugar, eggs, baking powder, cocoa powder and liqueur/coffee (if using) in bowl, and mix **15 sec/speed 7**.

Add reserved chocolate and almonds, and combine **20 sec/speed 6**.

Pour mixture into prepared tin and bake in centre of the oven for about **45 minutes** or until a skewer inserted into the centre comes out clean.

Allow to cool in tin for **20 minutes** then transfer to wire rack to completely cool.

Decorate with dusted icing sugar or *Chocolate Ganache*.
Recipe: page 70.

Torta Caprese - Flourless Chocolate Cake - Conventional

Makes one 15 cm round cake | Serves: 6-8 slices
Gluten free

Ingredients

50 g unsalted butter, diced, at room temperature

50 g sugar

2 eggs, at room temperature

2 teaspoon baking powder

2 teaspoon cocoa powder

1 tablespoon almond or coffee liqueur or strong coffee (optional)

80 g dark chocolate, grated

80 g almonds, finely chopped with a knife or chopped in food processor or crushed in a tea towel with a rolling pin

2 teaspoon icing sugar or cocoa for dusting

Method

Preheat oven **180°C** non-fan (**160°C** fan forced). Grease and line 15 cm round, spring form/loose bottom cake tin, and set aside. If not using a loose bottom tin, ensure that the lining extends up the side of the tin to allow easy removal of cooked cake.

In a mixing bowl, place unsalted butter and sugar, and beat until creamy, then add eggs, baking powder, cocoa powder and liqueur/coffee (if using), and mix until combined.

Add grated chocolate and finely chopped almonds, and mix until combined.

Pour mixture into prepared tin and bake in centre of the oven for about **45 minutes** or until a skewer inserted into the centre comes out clean.

Allow to cool in tin for **20 minutes** then transfer to wire rack to completely cool.

Decorate with dusted icing sugar or *Chocolate Ganache*.
Recipe: page 70.

Mindfully Enjoying

Eating is a great opportunity to practice mindfulness and to take the time to notice your food and your body. In just4Me, Caroline talks about nourishing your body and taking some me-time with a cuppa and a slice of cake. This practice of Mindfully Enjoying gives you space to notice your inner experience of eating.

Mindful eating helps us to learn to pay attention to our physical experience of eating and our inner experience as we nourish our bodies. Mindful eating can be practised with any food and is a moment to focus on your enjoyment, nourishment and fulfilment from food. It is not a time for self-criticism, shaming, judgement or guilt. In this mindful moment we practise having me-time and give ourselves permission to Mindfully Enjoy.

Once you have finished making your Torta Caprese and it is ready to eat, take a mindful moment to do this practice. Cut yourself a slice of the cake. You decide how much. Remember, this is a time to enjoy and nourish, not a time of restriction, over indulgence, or judgement. Find somewhere quiet to sit with your cake. Look at its colour; be curious. Take the time to notice all of its minor details. Are there variations in the tone? Is there a contrast in the icing versus the cake? Is it crumbly? Does it

look soft and moist? Be extremely curious. Take a small amount of the cake and bring it to your nose. Breathe in the rich, beautiful, complex smell of your Torta Caprese. What ingredients do you notice? Do you notice that you start to salivate? Eat the piece of cake. As you chew it, notice the taste, the sensations, the flavour, the texture.

Remember, no judgement about what you notice. Just notice it and taste it with mindful curiosity. As you take the next bite, again notice the colour, the shape, the texture. As you take bite after bite, notice all of your experience. Notice the softness, notice the richness, notice the sweetness, notice the bitterness, notice your enjoyment. Pause between each bite and give yourself permission to enjoy slowly, thoughtfully, intently. When you have finished, scan your body and notice how your body feels. Are you full? Are you still hungry? Trust yourself to know what your body needs and the signals it is giving you. With openness and compassion, listen to what your body is saying that it needs.

Traditional Boiled Fruitcake

My good friend, Lindy, gave me this recipe many years ago. This is one of the few cakes I made in my non-baker days. It reminds me of my Nana and the times I spent with her, and how her wisdom seemed to always make me feel okay with the world.

Although traditional in style, it's actually a light/golden fruitcake, more suited to modern tastes. However, it still has a feel of the old-fashioned fruitcake about it. Maybe it's the sherry! I make this as a square cake as it fits on my Nana's cake stand and seems traditional to me. Use a round tin if you don't have a small square tin.

Traditional Boiled Fruitcake - Thermomix

Makes one 15 cm round cake or 13 cm square cake
Serves: 6-8 slices

Ingredients

Peel of one lemon, yellow part
 only

40 g light brown sugar

60 g seedless raisins

50 g currants

40 g sultanas

120 g unsalted butter, diced

½ teaspoon bicarbonate of soda

½ teaspoon ground mixed spice

50 g sherry

40 g water

1 egg, at room temperature

140 g plain flour

1 teaspoon baking powder

15-20 nuts to decorate (pecans,
 walnut halves, blanched
 almonds)

1 tablespoon smooth apricot jam
 for glazing, once baked

Method

Preheat oven to **150°C** non-fan (**130°C** fan forced). Grease and line 15 cm round tin or 13 cm square cake tin, and set aside.

Place lemon peel and sugar in mixing bowl, and mill **5 sec/speed 10.**

Add dried fruits, butter, bicarbonate of soda, mixed spice, sherry and water. Cook **10 mins/100°C/reverse/speed 1.**

Allow to cool in bowl for **30-40 minutes**. (I put the bowl in the fridge. I have forgotten about it often, and once left it there for a few days, and all was fine. The flavour was wonderfully enhanced with the extra soaking time).

When mixture is cool, add egg, flour and baking powder, and mix **15 sec/reverse/speed 3.**

Pour into prepared tin and level. Decorate top with nuts.

Place in preheated oven and bake **50-60 minutes**. Check after **45 minutes.** Cake is cooked when a skewer inserted into the centre of the cake comes out clean.

Brush top with a little apricot jam to glaze while cake is hot and still in the tin. Cool in cake tin for **15 minutes** then turn onto rack to completely cool.

Traditional Boiled Fruitcake - Conventional

Makes one 15 cm round cake or 13 cm square cake
Serves: 6-8 slices

Ingredients

Zest of one lemon, yellow part
    only

40 g light brown sugar

60 g seedless raisins

50 g currants

40 g sultanas

120 g unsalted butter, diced

½ teaspoon bicarbonate of soda

½ teaspoon ground mixed spice

50 g sherry

40 g water

1 egg, at room temperature

140 g plain flour

1 teaspoon baking powder

15-20 nuts to decorate (pecans,
    walnut halves, blanched
    almonds)

1 tablespoon smooth apricot jam
    for glazing, once baked

Method

Preheat oven to **150°C** non-fan (**130°C** fan forced). Grease and line 15 cm round tin or a 13 cm square tin, and set aside.

Place lemon zest, sugar, dried fruits, butter, bicarbonate of soda, spice mix, sherry and water in a saucepan and cook **10 minutes** on **medium heat**. Take off heat and transfer mixture to a bowl.

Allow to cool in bowl for **30-40 minutes** (I put the bowl in the fridge. I have forgotten about it often, and once left it there for a few days, and all was fine. The flavour was wonderfully enhanced with the extra soaking time.)

When mixture is cool, add egg, flour and baking powder, and mix until just incorporated.

Pour into prepared tin and level. Decorate top with nuts.

Place in preheated oven and bake **50-60 minutes**. Check after **45 minutes**. Cake is cooked when a skewer inserted into the centre of the cake comes out clean.

Brush top with a little apricot jam to glaze while cake is hot and still in the tin. Cool in cake tin for **15 minutes** then turn onto rack to completely cool.

Mindful Wisdom: I Am Enough

When Caroline described to me that, for her, a Boiled fruitcake is a reminder of her Nana, and her Nana's wisdom that "everything is okay", it made me think of some wise words that someone once shared with me. You. Are. Enough. You, as you exist right now, are enough. You are enough to face your sadness. You are enough to help a friend. You are enough to get through that exam. You are enough to try baking a fruitcake for the first time. You are enough!

The practice of mindfulness teaches us to use our mind with intent, purpose, compassion and non-judgemental curiosity. Being able to focus our awareness in this way can help us to overcome even the strongest, oldest, and most destructive beliefs. Only with inwards attention can we start to become aware of our negative self-beliefs, their harm, and our desire to be free of them. This mindful moment is to help you practise paying attention, listening for your negative self-beliefs, and challenging them. Making a fruitcake takes time. Negative self-beliefs take time to develop too. Challenging them and dissolving them also takes time.

While you wait for your mixture to cool or for your fruitcake to bake, take a mindful moment to do this practice. Find a comfortable position, sitting or lying down. Let your eyes close and begin to notice your breathing. Notice the air flow in, and flow out. Be curious with your attention and just "notice" your breath. Give yourself permission to be still. In this moment all you need to focus on is being still.

As you find your peaceful centre, focus on you. Resist anxious movements that only distract you from your inner self. Just be still, it is okay. Bring all the pieces of you that have been scattered all over the place back together in this moment. You are enough.

The person you are noticing in this moment is enough. If part of your mind doubts this or yells criticism, or casts doubt, be still and breathe, knowing that you are enough. You are enough to receive care from others, you are enough to achieve your goals, you are enough to support yourself through struggles, you are enough to heal your pain, you are enough. Where you are broken, you are enough to heal yourself.

As you think these words to yourself, listen to the reply of your body and mind, with curiosity. Perhaps you notice that these words are powerful, or perhaps you notice they touch on some pain. Perhaps you notice that part of you wants to reject these words. With kindness and compassion just notice how these words of care feel. Before opening your eyes, take a moment to breathe in the words and take solace in the knowledge that you can return to this connection to yourself at any time.

Gently begin to move and bring movement back into your body. Open your eyes and take the peaceful wisdom with you as you return to your Boiled fruitcake and your piece of me-time.

'Hello Ginger!' Cake

This cake is for ginger lovers! Its use of three types of ginger give it a spicy warmth and depth of flavour. It's not overly sweet as it has a lot less sugary stuff than traditional ginger cakes.

Each type of ginger: fresh, ground and glacé says, "Hello." to your tastebuds at different stages of eating, keeping them dancing with delight. Ginger is known for its many heath properties, but I find its aid in calming most useful, and love this cake with a cup of green jasmine tea when I need to take a moment to calm down. Enjoy this cake and get ready for your tastebuds to say, "Hello Ginger!".

'Hello Ginger!' - Thermomix

Makes one 15 cm x 9.5 cm x 6.5 cm loaf cake | Serves: 6 slices
Gluten free if made with buckwheat

Ingredients

2 cm piece fresh ginger, peeled and roughly chopped

40 g glacé ginger

60 g coconut sugar (or brown sugar of choice)

2 eggs, at room temperature

150 g unbleached spelt flour or buckwheat flour (or plain white flour)

1 teaspoon ground ginger

½ teaspoon ground cardamom

½ teaspoon ground cinnamon

80 g plain yogurt

60 g olive oil

pinch of salt

2 teaspoon baking powder (or 1 teaspoon if using plain white flour)

20g shredded coconut, for topping (or Fast chocolate topping)

Method

Preheat oven **180°C** non-fan forced (**160°C** fan forced). Grease and line a 15 cm x 9.5 cm x 6.5 cm loaf tin, and set aside.

Place raw ginger, glacé ginger, and sugar in mixing bowl. Mill **10 sec/speed 9**.

Add eggs, and mix **30 sec/speed 4**.

Add flour, ground ginger, cardamom, cinnamon, yogurt, oil and salt. Mix **1 min/speed 5**.

While blades are running **12 sec/speed 5**, add baking powder through lid to ensure even distribution.

Pour batter into prepared tin and top with shredded coconut, if using, or leave plain if using Fast chocolate topping .

Bake for **30-35 minutes**. Cake is cooked when a skewer inserted into the centre of the cake comes out clean.

Leave to cool in tin for **5 minutes**, and then turn onto wire rack until completely cooled.

If using *Fast Chocolate Topping*, dress cake while it's still in the tin, and hot from the oven. Recipe: page 72.

Optional dressing: *Chocolate Ganache*. Recipe: page 70.

'Hello Ginger!' - Conventional

Makes one 15 cm x 9.5 cm x 6.5 cm loaf cake | Serves: 6 slices
Gluten free if made with buckwheat

Ingredients

60 g coconut sugar (or brown
    sugar of choice)

2 eggs, at room temperature

150 g unbleached spelt flour
    or buckwheat flour (or plain
    white flour)

1 teaspoon ground ginger

½ teaspoon ground cardamom

½ teaspoon ground cinnamon

2 cm piece fresh ginger, peeled
    and grated

40 g glacé ginger, finely chopped

80 g plain yogurt

60 g olive oil

pinch of salt

2 teaspoon baking powder

20 g shredded coconut, for
    topping (or Fast chocolate
    topping)

Method

Preheat oven **180°C** non-fan forced (**160°C** fan forced). Grease and line a 15 cm x 9.5 cm x 6.5 cm loaf tin, and set aside.

Place sugar in bowl with eggs, and mix until pale and creamy.

Add flour, ground ginger, cardamom, cinnamon, fresh ginger, glacé ginger, yogurt, oil and salt. Mix together on medium speed until creamy - approximately **2-3 minutes**.

While beaters are running, add baking powder, and mix briefly to ensure even distribution.

Pour batter into prepared tin and top with shredded coconut, if using, or leave plain if using Fast chocolate topping.

Bake for **30-35 minutes**. Cake is cooked when a skewer inserted into the centre of the cake comes out clean.

Leave to cool in tin for **5 minutes**, and then turn onto wire rack until completely cooled.

If using *Fast Chocolate Topping*, dress cake while it's still in the tin, and hot from the oven. Recipe: page 72.

Optional dressing: *Chocolate Ganache*. Recipe: page 70.

Mindful Emotions

One of the most difficult things about our emotions can be learning to allow them space, learning to be open to them, and learning to soften our resistance to them. When it comes to anger, people often see anger as being negative, destructive or undesirable.

We do not get to choose our emotions: we can only choose what we do with them and how we treat ourselves when we are experiencing them.

We feel anger for a very good reason: anger is our natural reaction to pain. If we can learn to use anger in a helpful way, anger can communicate to others how we would like to be treated.

This next mindfulness practice is my personal favourite for strong emotions such as anger. It was created by Kristin Neff and Chris Germer of the Center for Mindful Self-Compassion and they call it Soften-Soothe-Allow. The aim of this practice is to learn to allow, sooth, and soften around difficult emotions. In this practice you will be encouraged to allow yourself to feel a mild to moderate emotion. If at any time you feel panic or discomfort, return to your breath and focus on your breath. If you need to, open your eyes, and centre yourself in your familiar and safe surroundings.

In the last 15-20 minutes that your Ginger cake is baking, find a comfortable sitting position, preferably somewhere near the kitchen so you can smell the soothing scent of the ginger. Close your eyes and begin to turn your attention to your breath. Not forcing any change to your breath, simply bring your awareness to your breath. Observe yourself with gentle and curious compassion and give yourself permission to turn your attention inwards.

Allow yourself to recall a mild to moderately difficult situation, perhaps the reason you are choosing to take some me-time. Now think about the situation. What sensations do you start to notice? What emotional label would you give these sensations? Try to find the first, true underlying feeling about this situation. Is it anger? sadness? fear? Try to find the emotion that is underneath your discomfort. Then, with a gentle voice, welcome the emotion by calling its name: "That is anger", or "That is pain". How does your body tell you that you are angry? As you notice the areas of heat, tension, pain, or energy, begin to focus on softening these areas.

Find how your body is resisting the emotion and begin to soften around the edges. Take in a deep breath of the ginger. Begin to soften and allow the emotion to be there. You will still feel the emotion but try to decrease your resistance. Let the muscles become soft. There is no need to make the sensations go away, just allow them space and decrease your resistance to your emotion.

Breathe in the calming ginger smell. Place your hand over your heart and take a deep soothing breath in. Find some kind words for yourself, such as, "Oh my dear, I know the feeling is strong. It is ok. It is hard right now, but you will be ok". Allow the discomfort to be there and repeat to yourself, "soothe, soothe, soothe". Breathe in the calming ginger. Soothe, soften, it is ok. These words remind us that we are hurt and that we need care. Repeat this for as long as you need.

When you're ready, slowly open your eyes, let your awareness spread to the rest of your body and take the peace and calmness with you as you tend to your Ginger cake.

Jane's Best-ever Mississippi Chocolate Mud Cake

Given to me to copy from a well-loved, hand written original, was what my friend, Jane, promised, was a recipe for the best-ever mud cake. As a former Home Economics teacher and current owner of a catering business, Jane knows her cakes; and with whisky in it, how could this not be the best mud cake ever?

Jane's version makes a cake to feed the nation. Mine is perfect for me, and maybe some to share. Try it with just a dusting of cocoa powder or dressed up in chocolate ganache and see if you share the rating of 'best-ever'.

Jane's Best-ever Mississippi Chocolate Mud Cake - Thermomix

Makes one 15 cm round cake
Serves: 6-8 slices

Ingredients

130 g plain flour

1 teaspoon baking powder

pinch of salt

20 g cocoa, Dutched (plus extra
for dusting top: approx. 1
tablespoon)

75 g dark chocolate, in pieces

125 g unsalted butter, diced, at
room temperature

180 g sugar

125 g very strong black coffee (or
2 teaspoon instant coffee and
125 g hot water)

50 g whisky

1 egg, at room temperature

Method

Preheat oven to **160°C** non-fan (**140°C** fan forced). Grease and line a 15 cm round tin, and set aside.

Place flour, baking powder, salt and cocoa into mixing bowl, and mix **10 sec/speed 6**. Set aside and wipe bowl clean.

Place chocolate into mixing bowl, and grate 5 **sec/speed 8**.

Add butter, sugar, coffee and whisky, and heat **3 min/60°C/speed 2** or until butter and chocolate are melted.

Leave in bowl to cool until just warm (40°C). Approximately **10 minutes**. (I put it in the fridge in the mixing bowl.)

With blades running at **speed 3**, add flour mix through hole in lid.

Then add egg through hole in lid. Mix until just incorporated, approximately **5 sec/speed 3**.

Pour into prepared tin and bake in preheated oven for **1 hour** (check at **50 minutes**).

The cake is cooked when a skewer inserted into the centre comes out clean. This cake often has cracks in the top.

Leave in tin to cool for **15 minutes**, then turn onto wire rack until completely cool.

Serve with dusting of cocoa or top with whipped *Chocolate Ganache*. Recipe: page 70.

Jane's Best-ever Mississippi Chocolate Mud Cake - Conventional

Makes one 15 cm round cake
Serves: 6-8 slices

Ingredients

130 g plain flour

1 teaspoon baking powder

pinch of salt

20 g cocoa, Dutched (plus extra for dusting top: approx. 1 tablespoon)

75 g dark chocolate, in small pieces

125 g unsalted butter, diced, at room temperature

180 g sugar

125 g very strong black coffee (or 2 teaspoon instant coffee and 125 g hot water)

50 g whisky

1 egg, at room temperature

Method

Preheat oven to **160°C** non-fan (**140°C** fan forced). Grease and line a 15 cm round tin, and set aside.

Place flour, baking powder, salt and cocoa into mixing bowl, and mix until incorporated. Set aside.

Place chocolate into medium sized, heatproof bowl, and set over a saucepan of water. Heat water to a gentle simmer, ensuring water doesn't touch the bowl. Leave on heat until chocolate is melted.

Add butter, sugar, coffee and whisky, and mix, over heat until butter is melted. Leave in bowl to cool until just warm (**40°C**). Approximately **10 minutes**. (I put it in the fridge in the mixing bowl.)

When cooled, add flour mixture then add egg, mixing until just incorporated.

Pour into prepared tin and bake in preheated oven for **1 hour** (check at **50 minutes**).

Cake is cooked when a skewer inserted into the centre comes out clean. This cake often has cracks in the top.

Leave in tin to cool for **15 minutes**, then turn onto wire rack until completely cool.

Serve with dusting of cocoa or top with whipped *Chocolate Ganache*. Recipe page: 70.

A Moment of Gratitude

Part of being mindful in the present moment is being able to show gratitude to other living beings for the ways they positively contribute to our lives. When we are truly present in the moment, we can see and feel the beauty in the world.

As you increase your mindful practice you will become more purposefully aware and accepting of the present moment and the joy/anger/love/peace/fear that is part of your lived experience.

In thinking about this beautiful mud cake (which is my favourite-of-all-time mud cake) I thought it a good moment to practise gratitude for showing self-love, gratitude for taking me-time, and gratitude for the people in our lives who share wonderful things with us, like Jane, who shared her recipe with Caroline and now with all of you!

Practise this exercise in mindful gratitude before, during or after you have made Jane's Mississippi Mud Cake. Showing true gratitude is about noticing the beautiful detail of a moment, noticing how it positively contributes to your life, and noticing the warm, glowing feeling of love/care/pride/connection that it provides.

In this practice, focus on the experience of baking your cake and what it brings to you. You may find that your own things to be thankful for are different to what is written here. Find gratitude for yourself and for this cake in this moment. Notice your gratitude to yourself for making this choice today. Pay gratitude to your body for supporting you as you bake this cake. Feel gratitude for the ingredients that were available to you to make this cake. Turn your attention to the moments spent in preparing/baking/eating/sharing this cake, and the moments that stand out in your mind as precious enough to replay again and again.

Finally, recognize that you are the source of this goodness you gave to yourself. Acknowledge that you have given yourself me-time because you deserve it. Acknowledge the ways that you have added goodness to your life today.

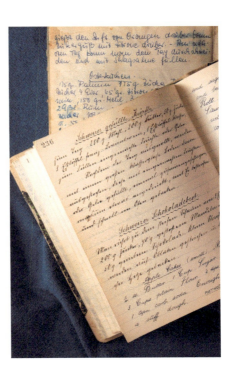

Date and Walnut Loaf

On my journey to find the perfect cake to go with my cuppa and me-time, I tested a lot of modern and traditional cake recipes. Hunting for inspiration in an old cookbook one day, I saw Date and Walnut Loaf, and was reminded that it was my Dad's favourite, which we used to have with lashings of butter when visiting his sister's house.

I always thought it difficult to make although I'm not sure why. To my surprise, it is one of the simplest cakes to make and bake. A bowl and spoon, no eggs, no dairy, and I've made it gluten free by using buckwheat flour. Super easy and suitable for everyone.

In my taste testing, this is the cake that was finished off first by both young and old alike.

You can make it without the walnuts, but I like their taste and I find it more enjoyable to get my omega 3 from walnuts rather than from fish oil capsules.

Date and Walnut Loaf

Makes one 15 cm x 9.5 cm x 6.5 cm loaf cake | Serves: 6 slices
Gluten free, dairy free, egg free

Ingredients

130 g pitted dates, roughly chopped

50 g walnut pieces, roughly chopped

60 g coconut sugar

3/4 tablespoon olive oil (or 1 tablespoon butter for dairy version or 1 tablespoon coconut oil)

1 teaspoon bicarbonate of soda

pinch of salt

230 g hot water

150 g wholemeal spelt flour or buckwheat flour

2 teaspoon baking powder.

Method

Preheat oven to **180°C** non-fan (**160°C** fan forced). Grease and line 15 cm x 9.5 cm x 6.5 cm loaf tin, and set aside.

Place dates, walnuts, sugar, oil, bicarbonate of soda, and salt in a bowl, and pour over hot water.

Allow to cool (about **30 minutes**).

When mixture is cool, stir in flour and baking powder until well incorporated.

Pour into prepared loaf tin and bake for **30–35 minutes**.

Cake is cooked when a skewer inserted into the centre of the cake comes out clean.

Allow to cool completely in tin.

Serve with butter or dairy free spread.

Object Mindfulness

Practising mindfulness is not something that has to take a long time. While it can be nice to have 30 minutes or an hour to quiet the mind and meditate, we can also give our brain small moments of stress relief in just a few minutes. Mindfulness is about learning the skills to quiet your mind, focus your attention, and observe things in the present moment without criticism.

To practise this, I have paired the Date and Walnut Loaf with a meditation exercise: focusing on an object. For this we will use the hero ingredient from the Date and Walnut Loaf, the walnut.

Before you begin baking, take a few walnuts in your hand. With curiosity, imagine that you have never seen a walnut before and want to learn all that you can about this unusual thing. Take that curiosity and sense of discovery with you throughout this exercise.

Begin to explore the walnut. What do your eyes see about this object? Notice its colour: are there variations in the tones? What colour would you label it? Explore what you see without judgement, assumptions or criticism. As you do this, if thoughts arise such as, "Why am I doing this?" or "People would think it is weird to do this." or "I don't have time for this." or "I hate walnuts.", acknowledge these thoughts but then bring your awareness back to the walnuts in your hand.

Notice the thoughts with curiosity.

Take one walnut and begin to explore its texture with your fingers. Does it feel soft? Does it feel firm? Do you notice if it is coarse or smooth? Perhaps you notice variations in texture, perhaps you observe that it is grainy or hard. Notice with curiosity. If at any time you notice intrusive or distracting thoughts, notice these too, and then bring your thinking back to what you set your mind to focus on in this present moment: the walnut.

Bring the walnut to your nose and notice the smell of it. Focus all your attention on this object in this moment. Be curious about where this walnut came from. Imagine the soil it grew in, the sun that shone to ripen it, the water that the farmer used to replenish it. Be curious about how this walnut came to be in your hand today.

Slowly bring the walnut to your mouth and become aware of the consistency, taste, sensation in your mouth as you chew. When you feel ready, make a mindful intention to swallow, noticing the feel of the walnut as it moves down your throat and into your stomach.

Take a moment to thank yourself for taking the time to notice this ingredient, this walnut. Think of all that it is as you continue your process of baking the Date and Walnut Loaf.

Jubilee Cake – Light Fruitcake

For some people it's not a cake unless it has fruit in it. This light fruitcake is a uniquely South Australian cake, created to celebrate the State's 100th anniversary in 1936, and has been a popular cake to have with a cuppa ever since.

It's the type of cake that keeps, and you can have it on hand for a midmorning tea break or if someone drops over. This is my take on the recipe used by my Dad's cousin, Toss. My version of Toss's cake has less sugar, makes only one loaf and is wonderful served with fresh butter. I've used fresh lemon zest in place of lemon peel for a brighter taste. This is a great cake to have with a cuppa on the go. Think football or anywhere where the thermos is taken.

Jubilee Cake - Light Fruitcake - Thermomix

Makes one 15 cm x 9.5 cm x 6.5 cm loaf cake
Serves: 6 slices

Ingredients

30 g sugar

½ lemon peel, yellow part only

40 g unsalted butter, diced,

50 g currants

50 g sultanas

125 g boiling water

150 g plain flour

1¼ teaspoon baking powder

pinch of salt

1 egg

Method

Preheat oven **180°C** non-fan forced (**160°C** fan forced). Grease and line a 15 cm x 9.5 cm x 6.5 cm loaf pan, and set aside.

Place sugar and lemon peel in mixing bowl, and mill **5 sec/speed 10**.

Add butter, currants, sultanas, and boiling water. Let stand until just warm, about **20 minutes**. This time allows the fruit to plump up. If I need my Thermomix bowl in the meantime, I tip the mix into another bowl to cool. When cool, I put it back in the Thermomix bowl to continue.

When fruit mixture is cooled, add flour, baking powder, salt and egg, and mix **5 sec/reverse/speed 4**.

Pour into prepared loaf tin and bake for **30-35 minutes**. The loaf is cooked when a skewer inserted in the centre comes out clean.

Cool for **5 minutes** in the tin then turn out onto cooling rack.

When cake has cooled, top with *Lemon Drizzle Icing* (recipe: page 73) and desiccated coconut.

Serve with butter. This cake keeps well in an airtight container at room temperature.

Optional dressing: *Icing Glaze*. Recipe: page 39.

Jubilee Cake - Light Fruitcake - Conventional

Makes one 15 cm x 9.5 cm x 6.5 cm loaf cake
Serves: 6 slices

Ingredients

30 g sugar

Zest of ½ lemon, yellow part only

40 g unsalted butter, diced,

50 g currants

50 g sultanas

125 g boiling water

150 g plain flour

1¼ teaspoon baking powder

pinch of salt

1 egg

Method

Preheat oven **180°C** non-fan forced (**160°C** fan forced). Grease and line a 15 cm x 9.5 cm x 6.5 cm loaf pan, and set aside.

Place sugar, lemon zest, butter, currants, sultanas, and boiling water in a large, heat proof mixing bowl. Let stand until just warm, about **20 minutes**. This time allows the fruit to plump up.

When fruit mixture is cooled, add flour, baking powder, salt and egg, and mix gently until all incorporated.

Pour into prepared loaf tin and bake for **30-35 minutes**.

The loaf is cooked when a skewer inserted in the centre comes out clean.

Cool for **5 minutes** in the tin then turn out onto cooling rack.

When cake has cooled, top with *Lemon Drizzle Icing* (recipe: page 73) and desiccated coconut.

Optional dressing: *Icing Glaze* (next page).

Icing Glaze

Ingredients

2 tablespoon icing sugar

1 teaspoon water

1 tablespoon coconut

Method

Place icing sugar and water in a small bowl, and stir with a spoon to form a paste. Spread over the warm cake and dust with coconut.

Noticing Anxiety: Mindful Body Scan

When we are anxious we experience the same physical responses that we feel in genuinely fearful situations: increased heart rate, shallow breathing, muscle tension, confusion and/or nausea. However, anxiety only occurs in situations in which we imagine danger when there really is none (e.g., thinking about an imagined future in which we falsely predict a bad or hurtful outcome). This exercise is designed to help you practise how to notice the physical signs of anxiety and how to begin to reduce them.

The quickest and most effective way to reduce the physical symptoms of anxiety is by slow, deep breathing. This body scan meditation is a very useful tool to help you focus on each part of your body with care, curiosity and non-judgemental attention.

Once you have placed your Jubilee Cake in the oven, set the timer for 30 minutes, and use the baking time to complete this body scan mindfulness practice. Begin by finding a comfortable seated position and allow your eyes to close. Take three long, deep breaths and begin to turn your attention inwards, and start to tune in to your body. If you become distracted by sounds in the environment, simply notice this, and then bring your focus back to your breathing. Focus your awareness on your feet and observe the sensations in your feet. Notice how they feel in your shoes or how they feel touching the floor. Do you notice any tension, tightness or discomfort? Notice this without judgement or concern. Take a few deep breaths and imagine you are sending the breath all the way down to your feet.

Next, move your awareness to your ankles, calves, and knees. With curiosity, observe the sensations you are experiencing. What do you notice, how would you describe it? Explore the sensations. Again, take a few breaths and imagine sending the breath down into your legs. If your mind begins to wander during this exercise, gently notice this without judgment and bring your mind back to focusing on your legs. Now move your focus to your thighs and buttocks. If you notice any discomfort, pain or stiffness, don't judge this. Just simply notice it. On your next exhale, allow your legs to relax. Allow them to be loose and heavy.

Next, bring your focus to your stomach and chest. What sensations do you notice here? How would you describe what you notice? Do you notice your clothing, do you notice your stomach churning or do you notice your stomach rising or falling with each breath? Next, notice your heartbeat and how your chest rises and falls during your breath. Let go of any judgments that may arise.

As we move through the body, bring your focus now to your shoulders, arms and hands. What do you notice? Do you notice a difference between your left and right arm? Shift your attention up to your neck and shoulders. What sensations do you notice? Do you notice tightness or rigidity? As you breathe, focus on identifying any tension and imagine it rolling off your shoulders.

Finally, bring your focus to all the parts of you; take a full, deep breath, grounding yourself in your body. Thank yourself for taking this time to centre yourself and for focusing on relieving your anxiety and tension. When you are ready, open your eyes, and return your attention to the present moment and your now baked Jubilee Cake.

Sweet Potato, Maple and Pecan Cake

This is the cake I turn to when I'm feeling flat and a bit drained. It looks and tastes like a treat, but is so packed full of goodness that my tired old body is recharged after my me-time. Like carrot cake, you can't taste the sweet potato, but your body gets the veggie goodness. I use buckwheat for flour as it's gluten free and high in protein and full of antioxidants and tastes nutty and yum. For the fat, I use olive oil; think good fats, and pecans for a little crunch and lots more vitamin and mineral goodness.

Finally, a little maple syrup for sweetness, and to spice up it all up: the warmth and sweetness of cinnamon and cardamom. This little cake is packed with so much goodness to refuel my tired body. Easy to make and bake, I always enjoy a little me-time meditation while it bakes, and I know I'm on the way to being revived.

Sweet Potato, Maple and Pecan Cake - Thermomix

Makes one 15 cm round cake | Serves: 6 slices
Gluten free, dairy free

Ingredients

50 g coconut sugar

peel of one orange, plus juice (approx. ½ an orange, 50 g)

100 g sweet potato, peeled and roughly chopped

2 eggs, room temperature

110 g oil of choice (olive, grapeseed, macadamia)

2 tablespoon maple syrup

110 g buckwheat flour (you can mill the buckwheat seeds in the Thermomix)

2 teaspoon baking powder

½ teaspoon bicarbonate of soda

50 g pecan nuts

1 teaspoon ground cinnamon

½ teaspoon ground cardamom

pinch of salt

8-10 pecan halves for topping (optional) or maple coated pecans

Method

Preheat oven **180°C** non-fan (**160°C** fan forced). Grease and line a 15 cm deep sided round tin, and set aside.

Place sugar and orange peel in mixing bowl, and mill **5 sec/speed 9**.

Add sweet potato, and grate **5 secs/speed 5**.

Add eggs, oil, maple syrup and orange juice, and beat **20 sec/speed 6**.

Add flour, baking powder, bicarbonate of soda, pecans, cinnamon, cardamom and salt, and mix **3 sec/speed 3**.

Pour into prepared tin and top with pecan pieces or maple coated pecans (if using).

Bake in preheated oven for **35-40 minutes**. Cake is cooked when a skewer inserted into the centre comes out clean.

Cool in tin for **20 minutes** then turn onto rack until room temperature.

For a party dressing, top cake with *White Chocolate, Cream Cheese Topping*. Recipe: page 74.

Sweet Potato, Maple and Pecan Cake - Conventional

Makes one 15 cm round cake | Serves: 6 slices
Gluten free, dairy free

Ingredients

50 g coconut sugar

zest of one orange, plus juice
    (approx. ½ an orange, 50 g)

2 eggs, room temperature

110 g oil of choice (olive,
    grapeseed, macadamia)

100 g sweet potato, peeled and
    grated

2 tablespoon maple syrup

110 g buckwheat flour

2 teaspoon baking powder

½ teaspoon bicarbonate of soda

50 g pecan nuts

1 teaspoon ground cinnamon

½ teaspoon ground cardamom

pinch of salt

8-10 pecan halves for topping
    (optional) or maple coated
    pecans

Method

Preheat oven **180°C** non-fan (**160°C** fan forced). Grease and line a 15 cm deep sided round tin, and set aside.

Place sugar, orange zest, eggs and oil into mixing bowl, and beat until fluffy and pale.

Add sweet potato, maple syrup and orange juice, and mix until incorporated.

Add flour, baking powder, bicarbonate of soda, pecans, cinnamon, cardamom and salt, and mix until incorporated.

Pour into prepared tin, and top with pecan pieces or maple coated pecans (if using).

Bake in preheated oven for **35-40 minutes**. Cake is cooked when a skewer inserted into the centre comes out clean.

Cool in tin for **20 minutes** then turn onto rack until room temperature.

For a party dressing, top cake with *White Chocolate, Cream Cheese Topping*. Recipe: page 74.

Maple Coated Pecans

This recipe makes more than you need for the cake but these are a great snack on their own, wonderful in a salad or perfect to top a cake.

Ingredients

150 g pecans

1 tablespoon maple syrup

Method

Preheat oven **180°C** non-fan (**160°C** fan forced). Grease and line a baking tray.

Place pecans and maple syrup into a bowl and mix to coat nuts evenly.

Spread maple coated nuts on baking tray and cook for **10 minutes** in preheated oven.

Allow to cool on rack. Store in an airtight container.

Sit and Let It Bake: Sitting Meditation

One of the things that people often say when attempting meditation or mindfulness is that it is too hard or too overwhelming to sit still and focus. So much of our lives these days are filled with things designed to distract us from our internal world; the radio, social media, television. This can make it feel unusual, uncomfortable and foreign to just sit and take time out.

Meditation and mindfulness are simple: we focus on ourselves, we dwell in the present, moment by moment, breath by breath. But your mind is not used to this quiet space; however, it is what your mind craves and needs in order to be revitalised and relaxed. Being present and switching off can take practise and it can be hard. This exercise is a sitting meditation to help you practise this skill. The more you practise the easier and more relaxing it becomes.

While your Sweet Potato, Maple and Pecan Cake is baking, find a comfortable sitting position either on a chair or on the floor on a cushion. Begin to focus on your breath and bring all of your awareness to your breath. Just monitor your breath, just breathe and pay attention. You will probably notice that part of you will get bored and not want to stay very long. You might notice your body or mind demands to shift or to do something else entirely. This is inevitable and it is not wrong…it will just happen. As soon as you notice, gently remind yourself you are practising a new skill, and focus back on your breath. As you sit, focus on the sensations of your breath. Notice how your stomach moves up and down with each breath. Notice as the air flows in your nose and down your airways. Notice as it returns out of your nose again. Just bring your awareness to your breath.

When your awareness goes somewhere else, just notice that you have lost attention and remind your brain that you are focusing on your breath and you are training yourself to be still. Recognise with praise and validation that catching yourself drifting off is a moment of awareness. This is what your mindfulness helps you practise. Noticing and refocusing. Practise this sitting meditation until your cake timer goes off.

Congratulate yourself for trying a new skill and for taking the time to learn how to focus your mind; and thank yourself for the stress relief and positive rewards that will follow from increasing your mindfulness.

Toscatårta – Almond Caramel Topped Butter Cake

A Swedish classic, Toscatårta is a butter cake topped with a delicious, crunchy and luscious caramel toffee mixed with almonds. Traditionally it's made more like a flan but I prefer it as a deep cake version. Plus, I don't need to find another tin; I use my faithful 15 cm round tin!

Don't let the extra step of making the toffee topping stop you from trying this cake. Even when the bake doesn't quite go to plan this cake is yum. I know; I had lots of test bakes to get the recipe just right, and while some were not pretty they all tasted amazing. Cut your perfectionist loose and enjoy this cake.

Toscatårta - Almond Caramel Topped Butter Cake - Thermomix

Makes one 15 cm round cake
Serves: 6 slices

Ingredients

110 g sugar

110 g plain flour

1 teaspoon baking powder

½ teaspoon salt

110 g unsalted butter, diced, at
    room temperature

2 eggs, room temperature

¾ teaspoon vanilla paste

Method

Preheat oven **180°C** non-fan forced (**160°C** fan forced). Grease and line a 15 cm round, spring form or loose bottom tin, and set aside. If you don't have a spring form/loose bottom tin, ensure the lining comes high up the sides to aid in removal of the cooked cake.

Place sugar into bowl and mill **5 sec/speed 10**. Scrape down sides.

Add flour, baking powder and salt, and **mix 5 sec/speed 4**.

Add butter, and whisk **30 sec/speed 4**. Scrape down sides.

Insert butterfly and add eggs and vanilla, then mix **30 sec/speed 4**.

Pour batter into prepared tin. Scoop out the centre a little to make an indentation. This helps flatten the top as the centre rises more than the rest of the cake.

Bake for **45-50 minutes**. Cake is cooked when a skewer inserted into the centre comes out clean.

About halfway through cooking time, start making *Caramel Almond Topping* (see next page).

Almond Caramel Topping - Thermomix

Ingredients

40 g unsalted butter

60 g light brown sugar

2 teaspoon plain flour

1 tablespoon milk

½ teaspoon sea salt flakes

½ teaspoon vanilla extract

80 g flaked almonds

Method

Place butter, sugar, flour, milk, salt and vanilla into mixing bowl, and heat without MC, **6 min/120°C (Varoma temp on TM31)/speed soft**. The mixture will thicken slightly.

Add almonds, and mix **10 sec/reverse/speed 1**. Set aside until cake is cooked.

Remove the cooked cake from the oven.

Increase temperature to **220°C non-fan (200°C** fan forced).

Carefully pour topping over cake in tin, being sure that all the top of the cake is covered.

Place cake back in oven on the upper shelf and cook for a further **5 to 10 minutes** until the topping is crisp and golden brown.

Allow to cool slightly in the tin before running a knife around the edge to separate the topping from the sides.

When cool enough to touch, gently remove the cake from the tin and allow it to cool completely on a wire rack before serving.

This cake keeps well in an airtight container for 3 to 4 days - if it lasts that long!

Toscatårta Almond Caramel Topped Butter Cake - Conventional

Makes one 15 cm round cake
Serves: 6 slices

Ingredients

110 g sugar

110 g plain flour

1 teaspoon baking powder

½ teaspoon salt

110 g unsalted butter, diced, at
    room temperature

2 eggs, room temperature

¾ teaspoon vanilla paste

Method

Preheat oven **180°C** non-fan forced (**160°C** fan forced). Grease and line a 15 cm round, spring form or loose bottom tin, and set aside. If you don't have a spring form/loose bottom tin, ensure the lining comes high up the sides to aid in removal of the cooked cake.

Place sugar, flour, baking powder and salt in bowl, and mix to incorporate.

Add butter, and mix, slowly at first, then at a medium speed until a creamy consistency is achieved.

Add eggs and vanilla, then mix on high speed until pale and creamy.

Pour batter into prepared tin. Scoop out the centre a little to make an indentation. This helps flatten the top as the centre rises more than the rest of the cake.

Bake for **45-50 minutes**. Cake is cooked when a skewer inserted into the centre comes out clean.

About halfway through cooking time, start making *Almond Caramel Topping* (see next page).

Almond Caramel Topping - Conventional

Ingredients

40 g unsalted butter

60 g light brown sugar

2 teaspoon plain flour

1 tablespoon milk

½ teaspoon sea salt flakes

½ teaspoon vanilla extract

80 g flaked almonds

Method

Place butter, sugar, flour, milk, salt and vanilla into a small saucepan, and heat over medium heat until mixture has thickened slightly. About **5 minutes.**

Stir in almonds, and coat well with mixture. Set aside until cake is cooked.

Remove the cooked cake from the oven.

Increase temperature to **220°C non-fan (200°C** fan forced).

Carefully pour topping over cake in tin, being sure that all the top of the cake is covered. Place the cake back in the oven on the upper shelf and cook for a further **5 to 10 minutes** until the topping is crisp and golden brown.

Allow to cool slightly in the tin before running a knife around the edge to separate the topping from the sides.

When cool enough to touch, gently remove the cake from the tin and allow it to cool completely on a wire rack before serving.

This cake keeps well in an airtight container for 3 to 4 days - if it lasts that long!

My Inner Critic is a Perfectionist: Compassion and Mindfulness

While writing the mindfulness practice for the Toscatårta, I caught myself being perfectionistic. I was not happy with what I was writing. I spent weeks thinking about it, trying to think of the perfect mindfulness exercise to accompany Caroline's cake. The amount of time that I resisted, reflected, thought, judged and threw away ideas was frustrating. My inner critic was active: "No, that's not good enough", "No, that is not exactly right", "See, you are not creative; you can't write".

It suddenly dawned on me. I had caught myself being perfectionistic and this perfectionism was only blocking my progress, my enjoyment, and my creativity. What an excellent moment of learning it was and now I hope to use it to pass on the learning to you also. This mindfulness practice is designed to help you practise noticing your inner critic and to start the process of ending the relationship with your inner critic.

Before you begin to bake the Toscatårta, read over this mindfulness exercise and take its words with you as you spend some me-time baking. Think back to the last time you made a mistake or think of something that you are feeling guilty about. What is it you are telling yourself that you did 'wrong'? As you think about this, notice how you treat yourself? What are the words that come to mind? What is it that you automatically thought about? Perhaps you thought, "Oh I am so embarrassed", or "I looked so stupid", or "I knew I couldn't do it". This is the voice of your inner critic. The harsh bully that comes up and kicks you when you're down.

The inner critic can attack you in many different ways: perhaps it convinces you that you are not worth taking care of, perhaps it convinces you that you deserve pain and suffering, perhaps it convinces you that you do not deserve to feel happy, or perhaps it convinces you that perfection is possible. In whatever form you hear it, notice it. What does this voice do to you? In the moment where you made a mistake, how did it make you feel? Did it help you? Was it on your side? What is the price of this internal harshness? The inner critic is the bully that tells you, "I told you so". In this moment, see if you can start to create some distance from the inner critic. Start to build some space between the critical voice and your caring self: recognise that as the caring person you are, of course you don't want to treat yourself with harshness.

Noticing the inner critic is the same as the other mindfulness skills we have been practising. It takes time and it is a new habit, but if you can catch it in the moment, create some distance, notice how punishing and unhelpful the inner critic is, then you can increase the space for your kind, supportive and compassionate self.

Lemon and Almond Cake from Santiago

The traditional Spanish Torta de Santiago (*cake of St. James*) has its origins in the Middle Ages. Still today, pilgrims and tourists who visit the great Cathedral of Santiago de Compostela in Galicia, where the relics of the apostle Saint James are believed to be buried, see the cake in the windows of every pastry shop and restaurant. It is usually marked with the shape of the cross of the Order of Santiago. I just dust the top all over with icing sugar.

It's traditionally made with blanched almonds, but I always make it with regular almonds, as that's what I always have in the pantry. With just four common ingredients it's easy to make, especially when you're in need of cake; feeling that the world is overwhelming you.

It's the cake that everyone always asks for the recipe; few ingredients, great flavour, gluten and dairy free, fast to make and bake, and easy to dress. This cake is easy to love!

Lemon and Almond Cake from Santiago - Thermomix

Makes one 15 cm round cake | Serves: 6 slices
Gluten free, dairy free

Ingredients

125 g almonds

80 g sugar

peel of a lemon, yellow part only

2 eggs, at room temperature

1 tablespoon icing sugar, for
topping

Method

Preheat oven **180°C** non-fan forced (**160°C** fan forced). Grease and line a 15 cm round, spring form or loose bottom tin, and set aside. If not using a spring form or loose bottom tin, ensure that the lining extends up the sides of the tin to allow for easy removal of the cooked cake.

Place almonds into mixing bowl, and chop **12 sec/speed 5**. Set aside.

Place sugar into mixing bowl, and pulverize **12 sec/speed 10**. Set aside one tablespoon for dusting.

Add lemon peel, and pulverize **5 sec/speed 10**.

Add eggs, and mix **2 min/speed 4**.

Add reserved almonds, and mix **3 sec/speed 3**.

Pour into prepared tin and bake in preheated oven for **20-25 minutes**. The cake is cooked when a skewer inserted into the centre comes out clean.

Allow to cool to room temperature in cake tin before transferring to serving plate and dusting with icing sugar.

Lemon and Almond Cake from Santiago - Conventional

Makes one 15 cm round cake | Serves: 6 slices
Gluten free, dairy free

Ingredients

80 g sugar

zest of a lemon, yellow part only

2 eggs, at room temperature

125 g almonds, finely crushed

1 tablespoon icing sugar for
    topping

Method

Preheat oven **180°C** non-fan forced (**160°C** fan forced). Grease and line a 15 cm round, spring form or loose bottom tin, and set aside. If not using a spring form or loose bottom tin, ensure that the lining extends up the sides of the tin to allow for easy removal of the cooked cake.

Place sugar, zest, and eggs into mixing bowl, and beat until pale and fluffy.

Add crushed almonds, and mix gently to fully incorporate.

Pour into prepared tin and bake in preheated oven for **20-25 minutes**. The cake is cooked when a skewer inserted into the centre comes out clean.

Allow to cool to room temperature in cake tin before transferring to serving plate and dusting with icing sugar.

Tune In, Pay Attention, and Choose: The Magic Quarter Second

Anxiety is something that everyone experiences. For some of us, we can easily cast it off and overcome it. For others, anxiety can quickly take hold and send us on a whirlwind of worry, adrenaline, and confusion. The difficult thing about managing anxiety is that anxious thinking enhances fear and makes everything seem overwhelming, dangerous, and too difficult.

This mindfulness practice is designed to help you practise how to notice anxious thoughts and practise creating space between your thoughts and your reactions. You may have selected the Lemon and Almond Cake from Santiago because you are feeling overwhelmed and craving something to ground you and comfort you.

Before making your cake, read this mindfulness practice and carry its message with you while your Santiago Cake is in the oven. Firstly, in dealing with anxiety, we need to recognise that anxiety is unhelpful and unproductive. More worry or anxiety will never result in less anxiety. In fact, anxiety affects our thinking and it hijacks our brain with stress hormones.

Secondly, we need to start to create space for ourselves. There

is a skill in being able to pause, notice anxiety, and start to create space for a new alternative path, rather than continuing down the path of worry and confusion. Researcher, Benjamin Libet, identified that the time between our brain having awareness of our intention to move and our brain enacting a movement is a quarter of a second. This space has been called "the magic quarter-second."

By catching our anxious thoughts (or any thought) in the magic quarter-second, we can interrupt our automatic or habitual responses and decide upon a new, healthier, wiser response (if any). This creates room for choice, and by practising mindfulness, we can increase our ability to tune in, notice, reflect, and choose.

So while your Santiago Cake is baking, see if you can focus on tuning in to yourself, paying attention to what thoughts you notice, reflecting on them with curiosity, and then making an active choice about what you want to do with those thoughts.

Remember, they are your thoughts and you have the power to choose whether to respond or not.

Half Orange Butter Cake

This citrusy cake is a great variation of a classic butter cake, with a wonderful sweet and sharp orange smell enriching the luscious butter taste. Citrus flavours always give me a lift, and I turn to this a cake often when I'm in need of a boost of energy.

Mandarins, as another option, give the cake a rich, sweet taste with an exotic fragrance. This is one of my all-time favourite cakes.

A great change up for this recipe is to use wholemeal spelt flour for more flavour and fibre or buckwheat flour for a gluten free option. To keep the lovely moist crumb, just add the juice from the remaining half orange, and one teaspoon more of baking powder. A little fresh ginger adds some heat, while adding a handful of nuts of your choice into the cake rather than on top is a tasty option for nut lovers. Choose a juicy orange with a thin skin. If you can only get thick pith oranges, use the zest and flesh only and not the bitter pith.

This cake keeps well and looks very glamorous, topped with orange slices or enrich it with my *Fast Chocolate Topping* (recipe: page 58) or go all out and top the cake for a party with *Chocolate Ganache* (see details below).

Like all butter cakes, it's better the day after for easy cutting, so it's good to plan ahead. However, I love its crumbly, just-baked texture and frequently eat it still warm.

Half Orange Butter Cake - Thermomix

Makes one 15 cm x 9.5 cm x 6.5 cm loaf cake
Serves: 6 slices

Ingredients

100 g orange with the skin on, cut in quarters (about ½ an orange)

110 g unsalted butter, diced, at room temperature

2 eggs, at room temperature

75 g sugar (optional 2 teaspoons for topping)

150 g plain flour (or wholemeal spelt or buckwheat flour)

1½ teaspoons baking powder (or 2 ½ teaspoons if using spelt or buckwheat flour)

½ orange, juice only (if using spelt or buckwheat flour)

½ orange, thinly sliced, for topping (optional)

8-10 pecans halves for topping (optional)

Options - to add to the cake mix

50 g pecans - milled 5 sec/speed 10 at the start, and set aside. To be added in with the flour.

2 cm fresh ginger, peeled - milled 5 sec/speed 10, added at the start with orange and butter.

Method

Preheat oven **180°C** (**160°C** fan forced). Grease and line a 15 cm x 9.5 cm x 6.5 cm loaf tin, and set aside.

Place orange quarters and butter into mixing bowl, and mix **10 sec/speed 8**. Scrape down sides.

Add eggs, sugar, flour, baking powder and juice (if using) then mix **20 sec/reverse/speed 4**.

Pour into prepared loaf tin, and top with orange slices and pecans, then dust top with 2 teaspoons of sugar (if desired).

Bake for **50 minutes** in preheated oven. The cake is done when a skewer inserted into the centre comes out clean, and the cake comes away from the sides.

Cool 5 minutes in the tin, then turn out onto a wire rack to completely cool.

Half Orange Butter Cake - Conventional

Makes one 15 cm x 9.5 cm x 6.5 cm loaf cake
Serves: 6 slices

Ingredients

This cake needs a food processor to make.

100 g orange with the skin on, cut in quarters (about ½ an orange)

110 g unsalted butter, diced, at room temperature

2 eggs, at room temperature

75 g sugar (optional 2 teaspoons for topping)

150 g plain flour (or wholemeal spelt or buckwheat flour)

1½ teaspoons baking powder (or 2½ teaspoons if using spelt or buckwheat flour)

½ orange, juice only (if using spelt or buckwheat flour)

½ orange, thinly sliced, for topping (optional)

8-10 pecans halves for topping (optional)

Options - to add to the cake mix

50 g pecans, roughly chopped, to be added with flour.

2 cm fresh ginger, peeled and roughly chopped, added at the start with orange and butter.

Method

Preheat oven **180°C** non-fan forced (**160°C** fan forced). Grease and line a 15 cm x 9.5 cm x 6.5 cm loaf pan, and set aside.

Place orange quarters and butter in food processor, and pulse until you have a creamy, orange mix but still with a bit of texture.

Add eggs, sugar, flour, baking powder and juice (if using), and mix briefly to fully incorporate all ingredients.

Pour into prepared loaf tin and top with orange slices and/or pecans, then dust top with 2 teaspoons of sugar (if desired).

Bake for **50 minutes** in preheated oven. The cake is done when a skewer inserted into the centre comes out clean, and the cake comes away from the sides.

Cool 5 minutes in the tin, then turn out onto a wire rack to completely cool.

Party Version

Topped with luxurious Chocolate ganache with a hint of Cointreau, this cake will be a welcome guest at any celebration.

Requirements for party version

Use a 15 cm round, high sided, spring form or removable bottom tin rather than a loaf tin. Line the sides to a few cm above the top of the tin.

Prepare as above, leaving cake top plain.

Bake as above and leave in the tin to cool completely. **Make** the *Chocolate Ganache* with the addition of a teaspoon of Cointreau. You will need **three times** the ingredients to create this dressing as in the photo. Recipe: page 70.

Gently pour over cake while in tin, and allow to cool completely; this can take a few hours, and you can put the cake in the refrigerator. When set, gently remove sides of tin and place cake on serving plate. Remove side baking paper.

Top with dried orange slices, either homemade in the oven or dehydrator or store bought. For a very fancy occasion, decorate with store bought chocolates such as Jaffas, Fruit Chocs and white yogurt balls.

Mindfulness of the Senses

In life we tend to gloss over the characteristics, nuances and intricate details of things in our lives. Often, we do this to make life simpler; however, it also means that we can miss the joy in small moments or take things of beauty for granted. This exercise involves bringing your attention to a single object and noticing its every detail. This not only helps you to practise focusing your mind and quieting your thoughts, but it is also good practise at finding the beauty in things.

Take the leftover orange in whatever form you have it (e.g., cut up or whole). Begin to explore the orange visually. See if you can describe what you see without judgment or interpretation. For example, "it is heavy" is a judgment but a more specific description would be "it weighs about 100 grams." Be specific. What do its different surfaces look like? How would you describe its shape to someone who cannot see it? How does the light illuminate off its surface? What colours do you see? Does it look smooth or bumpy? Does it look soft or hard? Does it look wet or dry?

Now take a few moments to notice its smell. What is it like to smell the piece of orange? How would you describe the smell of the flesh? How would you describe the smell of the

rind? Again, see if you can describe what you see without judgment or interpretation. Now, turn your attention to what it is like to hold the orange. How heavy would you describe it? Is it smooth or bumpy? Is it soft or hard? Does it feel wet or dry?

Carefully take the orange in your hand and squeeze the juice in to your other hand. What does it feel like to put pressure on the orange and squeeze it? What do you notice about your hand? What does the juice feel like? Is it cold? It is warm? Is it sticky? Finally take the orange and taste it with your mouth. What do you notice about the taste? How would you describe the texture? What do you notice happens in your mouth when you taste the orange? Once you have

finished exploring the orange, take a moment to acknowledge all the care and attention you just paid to this ingredient, this orange. Make a note to remember all of the small details of the orange and the impact it had on your senses: the smell, the look, the texture, the taste.

Think of all the details that you noticed and how much fuller the present moment is by paying attention to the details of this one object. Imagine how much fuller life would be if you took this much enjoyment from everything you see, hear, taste, touch or smell.

Coconut and Rum Kuranda Cake with Rum Syrup

This cake was inspired by my visits to the beautiful, tropical town of Kuranda in Far North Queensland. This small village, set in lush rainforest, is home to some dear friends.

With the nearby Atherton Tablelands, the home of coffee and tea growing in Australia, I thought a cake to celebrate the delicious ingredients from the area was a must in a collection of cakes to have with a cuppa.

This cake is rich with pecans, pineapple, muscovado sugar and Bundaberg rum, all from the tropical north.

Gluten free, moist and luscious, this cake always reminds me of the sunshine and warmth of Kuranda. I serve it with a generous spoonful of thick cream or yogurt on the side.

Coconut and Rum Kuranda Cake with Rum Syrup - Thermomix

Makes one 15 cm round cake | Serves: 6 slices
Gluten free

Ingredients

75 g polenta

100 g desiccated coconut

50 g pecans (plus a few to crush for topping)

a pinch of salt

1 teaspoon cinnamon

1½ teaspoon baking powder

40 g dark muscovado sugar

110 g butter

2 eggs, at room temperature

85 g tinned pineapple pieces (the contents of 225 g tin of pineapple, drained, the juice reserved for the syrup and a few pieces reserved for the topping)

Method

Preheat oven 180°C non-fan (**160°C** fan forced). Grease and line the base of a 15 cm round cake tin with baking parchment, and set aside

Place polenta in mixing bowl, and mill **10 sec/speed 10**.

Add coconut, and mill **10 sec/speed 10**.

Add pecans, salt, cinnamon, and baking powder, and mill **8 sec/speed 5**. Set aside.

Place sugar into mixing bowl, and mill **5 sec/speed 10**.

Add butter, and mix **30 sec/speed 6**.

With blades running at **speed 3**, add eggs through hole in lid, and stir for **6 sec**.

Add pineapple pieces and reserved polenta/coconut/pecan mixture, then mix **10 sec/speed 4**.

Pour into prepared tin and smooth the top level. Decorate top with reserved pineapple pieces and with a few crushed pecans.

Bake for **20 minutes** at **180°C** non-fan forced (**160°C** fan forced), then turn down the heat to **160°C** non-fan (**140°C** fan forced) for a further **20–30 minutes** or until the cake is firm. Total bake: **40–50 minutes** in a preheated oven. Cake is cooked when a skewer inserted into the centre comes out clean.

See syrup recipe on page 66.

Rum Syrup

Thermomix

Ingredients

100 g pineapple juice, reserved from tinned
  pineapple pieces*

30 g dark muscovado sugar

1 tablespoon brown rum

Method – syrup

Place reserved pineapple juice, dark muscovado sugar and brown rum into mixing bowl. Heat without MC, **8 min/100°C/speed 2** to make a thin syrup.

Spike holes, with a skewer, in the top of the cooked cake while it is still warm and in its tin. Ensure you push all the way to the bottom of the cake to allow the syrup to soak through the whole cake.

Then spoon over the hot syrup. Leave until almost cool, then lift out of the tin.

** If using fresh pineapple, add a large slice to 100 g of water, cook it for **10 minutes** at a simmer before bringing it to the boil. Use the pineapple-flavoured water in place of the juice from the tinned pineapple.*

Conventional

Ingredients

100 g pineapple juice, reserved from tinned
  pineapple pieces*

30 g dark muscovado sugar

1 tablespoon brown rum

Method – syrup

Place reserved pineapple juice, dark muscovado sugar and brown rum into small saucepan. Bring to the boil and simmer to make a thin syrup.

Spike holes, with a skewer, in the top of the cooked cake while it is still warm and in its tin. Ensure you push all the way to the bottom of the cake to allow the syrup to soak through the whole cake.

Then spoon over the hot syrup. Leave until almost cool, then lift out of the tin.

** If using fresh pineapple, add a large slice to 100 g of water, cook it for **10 minutes** at a simmer before bringing it to the boil. Use the pineapple-flavoured water in place of the juice from the tinned pineapple.*

Coconut and Rum Kuranda Cake with Rum Syrup - Conventional

Makes one 15 cm round cake | Serves: 6 slices
Gluten free

Ingredients

75 g polenta

100 g desiccated coconut

50 g pecans (plus a few to crush for topping)

a pinch of salt

1 teaspoon cinnamon

1½ teaspoon baking powder

40 g dark muscovado sugar

110 g butter

2 eggs, at room temperature

85 g tinned pineapple pieces (the contents of 225 g tin of pineapple, drained, the juice reserved for the syrup and a few pieces reserved for the topping)

Method

Preheat oven 180°C non-fan (**160°C** fan forced). Grease and line the base of a 15 cm round cake, and set aside.

Place polenta in a food processor, and pulse a few times.

Add coconut, and pulse a few times.

Add pecans, salt, cinnamon and baking powder, and pulse a few times. Set aside.

Place sugar and butter in a mixing bowl, and beat until creamy.

With beaters running at low speed, add eggs, one at a time, and mix until incorporated.

Add pineapple pieces and reserved polenta/coconut/pecan mixture, and beat until well combined.

Pour mixture into prepared tin and smooth the top level.

Decorate top with reserved pineapple pieces and with a few crushed pecans.

Bake for **20 minutes** at **180°C** non-fan (**160°C** fan forced), then turn down the heat to **160°C** non-fan (**140°C** fan forced) for a further **20-30 minutes** or until the cake is firm. Total bake: **40-50 minutes** in a preheated oven. Cake is cooked when a skewer inserted into the centre comes out clean.

See syrup recipe on page 66.

Stop and Smell the Roses: Walking Mindfulness

For the last recipe of the book I wanted to expand our practice from the kitchen activities to other areas. Walking mindfulness is a great way to bring awareness to an everyday activity. Find a moment when you are out walking, whether it is buying the groceries for this recipe, walking from the car, or just taking the time to go for a walk around the block and practise this exercise. Or, you could just imagine going for a walk. When I read about the Kuranda Cake I could not help but imagine tropical North Queensland, so perhaps you could imagine Kuranda.

As you begin your walk, allow yourself to fall in to a natural pace. Allow your arms to find a comfortable position and begin to pay attention to your body with each step you take. Notice with gently curiosity the lifting and falling of your feet. Notice the movement of your muscles in each leg. Notice your body moving or notice the reverberating sensation that each step sends through your body.

When your attention starts to drift, notice, "that is my mind becoming distracted", and gently bring your awareness back to the sensation of walking. As you walk, start to expand your attention to the sounds that you hear. Practice noticing these sounds without labelling or judging if they are pleasant or unpleasant. Just notice them, "that is a humming noise", "that is my ear hearing a whistling noise". Just notice, and notice what it is like to experience those sounds.

Shift your awareness to what you see. With curiosity, notice the colours and objects that you see. See if you can notice how you observe each object? Do your thoughts make a judgement? Are your thoughts critical? Do your thoughts take the object for granted? See if you can be curious about your observations.

With everything you experience with each sense while on your walk, keep an openness to experiencing this present moment. Enjoy the feeling of just being in this moment as you walk: there is nothing else to do, no better place to be, nothing to fix. It is just you paying attention to yourself and your present moment with full awareness.

As you finish your walk, bring your awareness back to your body, your muscles, your movements and the sensations of walking. Notice the lifting and falling of your feet. Notice your feet as they find the earth. Take a moment to thank yourself for practising mindfulness and for taking this time to revitalise your mind and pay kind attention to yourself.

Chocolate Ganache

I love chocolate ganache for dressing a cake as it has a lot less sugar than buttercreams yet feels very decadent, plus it is super easy to make.

Quality matters when dealing with chocolate. Your topping will only be as good as the chocolate you use. I use 70 % eating chocolate rather than cooking chocolate. As this cake is just for you it seems only right that you use the best chocolate you can afford.

Makes enough for one 15 cm cake.

Ingredients

100 g good quality, 70% dark chocolate, in pieces

35 g unsalted butter, room temperature

pinch of salt

1 teaspoon Liqueur (optional to suit cake, eg Kahlua for Torta Caprese or
    Cointreau for Half Orange Cake)

Thermomix

Place chocolate into mixing bowl, and grate **5 sec/speed 8**. Scrape down sides with spatula.

Add butter, salt and liqueur, if using, and melt **1-2 mins/50°C/speed 3**. If all chocolate is not melted heat another minute at **50°C/speed 3**.

Allow ganache to cool a little to a thick, pouring consistency.

Place cooled cake on a wire rack over a baking tray. Pour the ganache on top, allowing it to run down the sides.

When pouring on cooled cake, tip the whole cake to ensure an even covering rather than using a knife to spread. This will ensure a smooth, glossy top.

Decorate with fresh berries or nuts of choice.

Conventional

Place chocolate into a mixing bowl over a saucepan of gently simmering water, to melt.

When melted, remove from heat and add butter, salt and liqueur, if using, and mix until combined

Allow ganache to cool a little until it's at a thick, pouring consistency.

Place cooled cake on a wire rack over a baking tray. Pour the ganache on top, allowing it to run down the sides. When pouring on cooled cake, tip the whole cake to ensure an even covering rather than using a knife to spread. This will ensure a smooth, glossy top.

Decorate with fresh berries or nuts of choice.

Fast Chocolate Topping

This is a great way to top a cake with chocolate in a hurry. Created by a very busy friend of mine, Karen Harris, in a moment of cake crisis; it has now become the 'go-to' topping of many of her friends. Thanks for your creative thinking, Karen! It is best made with good quality, dark chocolate, but in a crisis any chocolate you have will be OK.

Ingredients

100g 70%, dark eating chocolate, finely grated (or milled in Thermomix or food processer)

Method

Cover top of hot cake in tin with a generous coating of milled chocolate.

Leave for **5 minutes** to begin to melt.

Smooth with the back of a spoon working in a circular motion, starting at the centre moving to the outer edge.

Allow to cool completely before removing from tin.

Drizzle Icing

Ingredients

80 g icing sugar

4 teaspoon orange juice/lemon juice/water/
    orange blossom water/rose water

Optional

Substitute 2 teaspoon of liquid with 2 teaspoon of liqueur
    of your choice (Grand Marnier or Cointreau, whisky)

Method

Place icing sugar in bowl and slowly add liquid, stir gently with a spoon until you have a smooth paste.

Pour over cooled cake.

Cinnamon Topping

This simple topping makes an elegant cake
that reminds me of my childhood.
Recipe is enough for one 15 cm x 9.5 cm x 6.5 cm loaf cake.

Ingredients

1 tablespoon sugar

½ teaspoon ground cinnamon

1 teaspoon unsalted butter

Method

Mix sugar and cinnamon together in a small bowl.

Rub unsalted butter over hot cake while still in tin. Then sprinkle sugar mix evenly over the cake top. Allow to cool in tin.

White Chocolate, Cream Cheese Topping

Sounds decadent and it is. With white chocolate, cream cheese and a little butter, this smooth, slightly tangy icing is just the thing when you feel like a little extra treat.

I was never one for cream cheese icing, however, this recipe has turned me into a cream cheese icing lover. It's the topping my friends always request when I bring cake to a function. Plus, my version has a lot less sugar than traditional recipes. Simply cover the cake and add a few nuts for a 'Company's Coming' topping or pipe roses on the cake for a party dressing. Whichever way you use the topping, I know you'll enjoy the treat!

Perfect on Sweet Potato, Maple and Pecan Cake or on "Hello Ginger!" Cake or Butter Cake or…

Thermomix

Makes enough for one 15 cm cake

Ingredients

20 g sugar

40 g white chocolate, broken in small cubes

25 g unsalted butter

150 g cream cheese

1 tablespoon orange juice

Method

Place sugar in bowl, and mill **8 sec/speed 10**. Set aside.

Place white chocolate into mixing bowl, and grate **8 sec/speed 8**.

Add unsalted butter, and melt **3 min/50°C/speed 3**.

Add cream cheese, orange juice, and milled sugar, and blend **30 sec/speed 3**.

Cover cooled cake with topping and set in refrigerator for **15 minutes**.

Make three times the recipe if piping roses.

Conventional

Makes enough for one 15 cm cake

Ingredients

40 g white chocolate, broken in small cubes

25 g unsalted butter, diced, at room temperature

150 g cream cheese, room temperature, roughly chopped

1 tablespoon orange juice

20 g icing sugar

Method

Place white chocolate into a heatproof bowl over gently simmering water, and allow to melt. Ensure no water touches the bowl.

Add unsalted butter, and, still over heat, gently stir until fully combined.

Remove from heat and add cream cheese, orange juice and sugar, and beat well with mixer until fully incorporated and creamy.

Cover cooled cake with topping and set in refrigerator for **15 minutes**.

Make three times the recipe if piping roses.

About Caroline W. Rowe

> Caroline W Rowe is an educator, author and Thermomix fan, who is enhancing the lifestyles of those who cook just for themselves because she strongly believes the "Me" is worth it.

As the manager of a household of one, (like nearly 25% of the households in Australia), Caroline is passionate about the importance of taking care of 'just Me' and has spent the last 6 years developing strategies, recipes and tips for managing a small household to prevent boredom, food waste, and overeating. She shares this information on her website Cookingjust4Me.com.

In 2014 she wrote the highly successful *Cooking for You and Me* cookbook for Thermomix. Then following her passion to find the perfect cake to go with a cuppa, she founded the just4Me Bake Club, an online cooking school with a collection of over 30 cake recipes supported by video tutorials. All the recipes are designed for small households. In *The Power of Baking with Mindful Intent* she shares some of her favourite Bake Cake recipes.

Prior to following her passion for just4ME cooking, Caroline worked in both marketing management and academic roles at the University of South Australia for nearly 20 years. She co-authored the popular marketing text book *Marketing Making the Future Happen*. Between her academic and marketing roles at the university, Caroline built a successful marketing consultancy business that she later sold to one of the major global advertising companies.

About Dr Susan L. Rowe

Dr Susan L. Rowe is a registered psychologist and mental health researcher. She is the co-owner and Director of mindhack, a psychology clinic on the Gold Coast, Queensland. Susan is also a clinical team member of Griffith University Psychology Clinic and is involved in a number of research projects.

Susan began her clinical career working with vulnerable children and families and broadly her career has focused on helping patients affected by stress and trauma. Susan has worked as a psychologist for 11 years in a range of settings including not-for-profit organisations, private practice, and for corporate businesses. Susan has extensive experience in treating children and adults affected by trauma and in 2015 she completed her Doctor of Philosophy on the study of resilience throughout the lifespan. Susan predominantly works as a psychologist in private practice while also providing training, supervision and lectures for other health professionals.

Susan is a Member of the Australian Psychological Society as well as several international associations. Susan is passionate about providing effective psychological treatment that is accessible to all members of the community. Susan practises the healthy lifestyle principles that she teaches her patients and she enjoys yoga, sunshine, exercise, coffee and quality time with her family and friends.

Resources - Mindfulness

If you would like to continue to expand your practice of mindfulness, or you would like to know more, here are some useful resources.

1. For more information about Mindfulness-based Stress Reduction here is the website for the Center for Mindfulness at the University of Massachusetts Medical School https:/www.umassmed.edu/cfm/

2. You can look for a Mindfulness-based Stress Reduction course in your local area or Palouse Mindfulness runs a free 8-week online course in Mindfulness-based Stress Reduction with tutorials, readings, and video-based learning. See here https://palousemindfulness.com/

3. Tara Brach, PhD, is a clinical psychologist who teaches a combination of Western psychology and Eastern spiritual practices. She has published a series of books about self-acceptance, compassion, and freedom from suffering. She also has a podcast and meditation downloads, https://www.tarabrach.com/

4. The Center for Mindful Self-Compassion is run by Kristin Neff, PhD and Christopher Germer, PhD, who also wrote the Soften Soothe and Allow meditation that inspired the activity on page 26. If you want to know more about self-compassion, see their website https://centerformsc.org/

5. For research and information on the benefits of mindfulness and meditation see the National Institute of Health (https://nccih.nih.gov/health/meditation), Health Direct (https://www.healthdirect.gov.au/mindfulness-and-mental-health), or The Conversation (http://theconversation.com/au/topics/mindfulness-463)

If you are experiencing symptoms of anxiety, depression, stress, grief or emotional ups and downs that lasts for more than two weeks, be sure to see your General Practitioner or in Australia call:

Lifeline 24 hours 7 days **13 11 14**

Blue Knot Trauma Helpline 9am–5pm 7 days **1300 657 380**

Health Advice Line 24 hours 7 days **1800 022 222**

Resources - Baking

Where to find the right cake tin

I used the following cake tins for all the recipes in this book and the *just4Me Bake Club*:

Round - Lakeland loose based 15cm round PushPan cake tin. It is a deep side tin and useful for all types of round cakes. I bought it from Lakeland at the Good Guys in Australia. Lakeland products are available in Australian online from the Good Guys and in the UK from Lakeland online. Other online cake suppliers and Amazon also stock this size round tin.

Loaf tins are a bit hard to find and are less standardised. The one I use is a small bread tin from US brand Fat Daddies. I like the deep straight sides. It is their Anodized Aluminium bread pan straight sided loaf 6 1/3" x3 3/4" x 2 2/3". I brought it online from an Australian cake supplier MyDreamCake.com. It is also available on Amazon. However, you can use other similar sized loaf tins such that major online baking suppliers including Lakeland sell.

Like more cake recipes?

Then visit the *just4Me Bake Club* and find out more about the Bake Club Collection of over 30 recipes, all supported by video tutorials.

www.just4MeBakeClub.com

www.facebook.com/
just4MeBakeClub/

www.instagram.com/
just4mebakeclub/

Wondering what to cook for dinner?

Like some tips for cooking for a small household? Then visit the *Cookingjust4Me* facebook page.

www.facebook.com/Cookingjust4me/

Printed in the United States
By Bookmasters